"I have read the messages received by Mary Kuhn from Our Lord and His Mother and addressed 'For My People' and 'For My Priests.'

What impressed me is that they are consistent with those received by the children of Fatima. The themes in the messages addressed 'For My Priests' are consistent with the theology of Pope Francis: Priests should not worry about material things, buildings, etc., but rather concentrate on prayer, reaching out to parishioners in need, encouraging people to spend time in prayer, etc.

I have known Greg and Mary Kuhn for 35 years, and I know they are sincere, devout Catholics. As to the authenticity of the messages, we must leave it to the judgment of Holy Mother Church. Anyone who reads these messages will be challenged! Sometimes they "hit a nerve"! It's good to be reminded of these essential aspects of our spiritual lives for our own good and that of the Church and world in which we live."

Fr. Ignatius Harrington,
Holy Resurrection Church;
Westerville, OH;
Melkite Greek Catholic Church

Messages from Heaven: For My Priests is a call to holiness! The entrance antiphon for the Mass of Pastors proclaims, 'Your priests, O Lord, shall be clothed with justice; your holy ones shall ring out their joy' (Psalm 132:15). Priestly abandonment to the call of holiness, like King David dancing before the Ark of the Covenant with abandon (2 Samuel 6:14) turns the mourning of God's people to joy-filled gladness and dancing (Jeremiah 31:13).

According to God's plan, priests and all the members of the Church have been called to holiness by the grace of Jesus

Christ. May the work by Mary and Greg Kuhn help our brother priests to pursue the Lord and embrace the call of holiness, following ever after until the day we all stand before the throne of God."

Father Todd Schneider,
Pastor of Assumption of the Blessed Virgin Mary;
Morris, Minnesota;
Roman Catholic Diocese of Saint Cloud

MESSAGES FROM HEAVEN: FOR MY PRIESTS Vol. I

"A priest goes to Heaven or a priest goes to Hell, with a thousand people behind."

~ *Saint John Marie Vianney*

MESSAGES *from* HEAVEN:
For My Priests
VOL. I

Compiled by
Greg and Mary Kuhn

Edited by
DeAnna Parks

The Order of Suffering Hearts, Inc.
Saint Cloud, MN 56304

Nihil Obstat: Rev. Robert Harren, STL, Censor Librorum

The Nihil Obstat is an official declaration through the Roman Catholic Church that a publication contains no doctrinal or moral error. It is not an endorsement of the content or views expressed.

Copyright © 2020 by The Order of Suffering Hearts

All scripture quotations are taken from The Holy Bible.

Some names have been changed or omitted to protect the identities of the persons involved.

Trade Paperback ISBN: 978-0-9986313-3-2
eBook ISBN: 978-0-9986313-4-9

Cover design by: Rev. Aaron Kuhn and DeAnna Parks
Editing and formatting by: DeAnna Parks

All rights reserved. No part of this book may be reproduced or transmitted in any form or by any means, electronic or mechanical, including photocopying and recording, or by any information storage and retrieval system, without permission in writing from the publisher.

Published in the United States by
The Order of Suffering Hearts

Printed in the United States of America
2020

10 9 8 7 6 5 4 3 2 1

SPECIAL SALES
Most O.S.H. books and media are available at special quantity discounts when purchased in bulk by corporations, organizations, and special-interest groups. For more information, please go to www.SufferingHearts.org.

PUBLISHED BY
THE ORDER OF SUFFERING HEARTS
Saint Cloud, Minnesota

MADE IN THE U.S.A.

For God's Priests

Contents

FOREWARD 11

PUBLISHER'S NOTE 19

INTRODUCTION 21

NOTE FROM THE SCRIBE..........................25

1993 - 1994 27

1995 - 1998 45

2000 - 2016 61

ACKNOWLEDGEMENTS 91

ABOUT THE AUTHORS 93

Foreword

My dear brother priests,

I wish to address two questions in this Foreword: (1) Are these messages legitimate? And (2) why should I read them?

Whenever anyone approaches me with alleged mystical experiences of private revelation my spiritual skepticism sends a warning to my mind: "the Church decides if private revelation is true, not me or you." A book like *Messages from Heaven: For My Priests* likely raises similar concerns in your own mind. Is it okay for me or my parishioners to read? How do we reconcile the contents of such messages against the public revelation of sacred scripture and magisterial teaching? In other words, are they legitimate?

Foreword

Here are a few principles of our Catholic faith to aid in your discernment. It is important to remember them when anyone claims to have private revelations from Heaven:[1]

1. The full, definitive and perfect *public* revelation of God's Word for our salvation is Jesus Christ, as preserved and articulated through Sacred Scripture. There is no new public revelation that will be expected before the Lord returns in glory.

2. Authentic *private* revelation is understood as God (or a soul or angel on God's behalf) supernaturally speaking to someone in this post-apostolic age. It never contains any "new" revelation of God for the sake of salvation of souls that has not already been revealed in the public revelation of God, but it may re-present the same truth, as when our Blessed Mother Mary presented herself as the "Immaculate Conception" to Saint Bernadette of Lourdes, France in 1858, four years after it was declared a dogma by Pope Pius IX.

3. To be authentic, claims of private revelation must ultimately be united perfectly to the Truth—Jesus Christ—and without contradiction to His public revelation. Thus, the authority of the Church is the one to decide the authenticity of private revelations. The Holy See has a thorough evaluation process and usually waits to authenticate alleged private revelation until after the locutions have ceased, often after the recipients are also deceased. For example, this is why the apparitions at Fatima to the three children in 1916-1917 were declared authentic in 1930 even while one of the children was still alive, but the alleged ongoing apparitions of Medjugorje (1981-present) have not, at least as of the print of this book.

---

[1] The Catechism of the Catholic Church, 65-67.

The legitimacy of these *Messages from Heaven: For My Priests* will not likely be authenticated for some time after I write this, since my mother (the Scribe) says that she continues to receive new messages and have locutions with the Lord, Mary, and a number of angels, saints, and souls on a daily basis. I pray that the lack of proof of authenticity does not deter you from reading them. I will also not try to convince you of their veracity. I hope that you will read them for what they claim to be: insights into the mind of God relative to our present moment in history. An analogy of *highlighting* may prove helpful.

Have you ever read a book that someone else has read and noticed personalized highlights of sentences, or glosses and notes in the margins? Have those highlights ever inspired you to concentrate more on the meaning of those noted texts, in a way that you otherwise might have skimmed passed? The private insights or revelations to the previous reader have somehow brought renewed emphasis on what was already present in the original public text.

This is much like how Heaven is revealed to us through the private revelation of God to an individual, whether by direct conversation with our Lord, an angel, a saint from heaven, or a soul in purgatory. The famous *Dialogue* between Jesus and Saint Catherine of Siena (14th century, Italy), the apparitions of Our Lady of the Immaculate Conception to Bernadette at Lourdes (19th century, France), and the plentiful encounters of souls from purgatory to Saint Padre Pio in San Giovanni Rotondo (20th century, Italy) are just a few historical examples in the life of the Church where heavenly locutions have highlighted the already established public revelation of Jesus Christ. They point us to Jesus in a renewed way. They say nothing new for our salvation, yet they re-present the mystery of God's constant intervention in history.

Foreword

The tone of voice in the *Messages From Heaven: For My Priests* is of Jesus, the Sorrowful Heart. Devotion to the Sacred Heart of Jesus is widespread in the world in part because the Lord knows of our human longing for His sacred love, which emanates from his Sacred Heart. In these Messages, though, the Sorrowful Heart of Jesus agonizes especially for the conversion of priests' hearts to heroic holiness. He reminds us that we are called to the holiness that is usually read about in sacred scripture and stories of the saints. God expects heroic holiness as the norm, not the exception, which may seem daunting, but should not be surprising. God asks us to see ourselves through His eyes, with the capacity for heroic sanctity, not through our limited self-vision.

I can remember an old woman, hard-of-hearing, who after one of my homilies remarked loudly to the person next to her, "I think he wants us to be saints." At the time, I imagine she was sarcastically referring to the homily that I had just given, as if I were expecting too much of average parishioners for an ordinary weekday in Ordinary Time. What I have learned over time is that most people do not have a reference point for heroic holiness in ordinary life, other than story book notions of inaccessible saints. Heroic holiness is so rarely lived that it often seems mythical and unrealistic. Read the biography and writings of any saint and one element becomes clear: God expects more of us than we expect of ourselves. Saints make the effort and set the example for others.

"Holiness demands heroism, heroism of a severe and difficult kind." – Medieval adage, referred to in *Catherine of Siena*, by Sigred Unset.

The *Messages from Heaven: For My Priests* will highlight how much God yearns for us to embrace the priesthood with the intensity and passion of a hero, like his saints in previous generations. At our ordination, the bishop asked us, and we responded:[2]

> *Are you resolved, with the help of the Holy Spirit, to discharge without fail the office of the priesthood in the presbyteral order as a conscientious fellow worker with the bishops in caring for the Lord's flock?* **I am.**
>
> *Are you resolved to celebrate the mysteries of Christ faithfully and religiously as the Church has handed them down to us for the glory of God and the sanctification of Christ's people?* **I am.**
>
> *Are you resolved to hold the mystery of the faith with a clear conscience as the Apostle urges, and to proclaim this faith in word and action as it is taught by the Gospel and the Church's tradition?* **I am.**
>
> *Are you resolved to maintain and deepen a spirit of prayer appropriate to your way of life and, in keeping with what is required of you, to celebrate faithfully the liturgy of the hours for the Church and for the whole world?* **I am.**
>
> *Are you resolved to exercise the ministry of the word worthily and wisely, preaching the Gospel and explaining the Catholic faith?* **I am.**
>
> *Are you resolved to consecrate your life to God for the salvation of his people, and to unite yourself more closely every day to Christ the High Priest, who offered himself for us to the Father as a perfect sacrifice?* **I am, with the help of God.**

---

[2] Rite of Ordination of a Priest (1968).

Then, in part of the prayer of consecration, the bishop prayed over us:

> *Almighty Father, grant to this servant of yours the dignity of the priesthood. Renew within him the Spirit of holiness. As a co-worker with the order of bishops may he be faithful to the ministry that he receives from you, Lord God, and to be to others a model of right-conduct.*

Of course, it is possible to read into the promises and prayers of ordination a kind of mediocrity or minimalist interpretation of how much is asked of us as priests. None of us intend to live that way, but if we are honest, it is easy to do. We should ask ourselves, is this the mind of Christ? Were we called to a casual priesthood that gets through the daily work like any other profession? Or is that desire in my heart for holiness more than a desire, maybe even an invitation of grace?

Read this book and see what image of holiness and priesthood is expressed in the *Messages from Heaven*. Then, when you are reading the scriptures in preparation for the celebration of Holy Mass or praying the Divine Office, see if the voice of God is any different in the Prophets of the Old Testament, or the Apostles in the New Testament. Most importantly, listen for the voice of Jesus in the gospels, and hear him call us to demands of discipleship that sound radical and uncomfortable.

God's call of conversion to holiness is not meant only for our personal betterment. Children learn ideas of what God the Father must be like through their experience of their earthly fathers. The disciples of Jesus marveled at Jesus' rapport with the Father, because they had never before seen someone act and pray like Him. So too, in our day, many fathers do not know how to model holiness for their children because it was not modeled for them. How will God's people know what a deep relationship with God looks like unless we step out and model it for them, like the saints? This is the conversion of heart of what Jesus once spoke when He walked this earth.

Why should I read this book? Because, the Lord still speaks today.

Father Aaron Kuhn
Founding member of the Order of Suffering Hearts
Priest of the Diocese of Saint Cloud, Minnesota
Son of the Scribe

Publisher's Note

Thank you for taking the time to prayerfully read this book. We want you to know that we took extreme care of these Messages from Heaven so as to preserve their authenticity, while trying to edit them for grammar and organize them for print.

Therefore, you may find certain terms or grammar are colloquial or easier to understand in spoken, rather than written, form. Please do not be discouraged. This was done intentionally, as the voice of Our Lord, Blessed Mother, and others from Heaven, were originally recorded on paper to reflect where they paused, what they emphasized, etc. It may take a little reading to become used to how it was recorded.

Furthermore, only slight punctuation has been added by the publishers, through the permission of Greg and Mary Kuhn, to allow for clearer understanding as to the meaning of a phrase or sentence.

Publisher's Note

We hope now, that you will enjoy these Messages from Heaven as dearly as we have.

The Publishers
The Order of Suffering Hearts
May 1, 2018

Introduction

Despite her horrific childhood, Mary Kuhn has always been a woman of faith.

She was raised in a very poor, Catholic family, the eldest daughter and second child of eleven children. Her mother was extremely unhappy, and often took it out on her family by way of physical and psychological abuse.

Mary's father often turned to alcohol to escape his miserable wife. In addition to this, Mary had acute asthma, which hospitalized her several times a year.

Yet, through it all, the Lord had a very strong influence in Mary's life. Mary was only three years old when she adopted the Blessed Mother as her own.

Her love for prayer started at an early age, and she often found solace in it. Jesus and the Blessed Mother were her friends and companions. She spoke with them, just as we speak to each other, and she would hear their Heavenly voices.

Introduction

Though she seldom spoke of it, she expected most others to have similar experiences with Heaven, even if they did not speak of it.

For my part, I was raised in a Catholic home, with three older brothers and one younger sister. My parents were solid, self-educated, hard-working dairy farmers in a very small town. Prayer was a common occurrence through a daily rosary and meal prayers, along with weekly Sunday mass and going to Catholic school.

Though my upbringing was much more peaceful than Mary's, tragedy was no stranger. My mother suffered greatly through the loss of three children – two born prematurely and a daughter, Mary Jane, who, at the age of nineteen, died of Lupus. Then, while bearing the loss of their daughter, I watched as my parents took in their daughter's newly born child, caring for it as if it were their own.

By age 18, farm life felt too restrictive for me, and, by God's mercy, I was able to leave and attend college.

It was shortly thereafter that I met Mary. We were both attending the same university, and on one particular evening, I happened upon a concert in which Mary was playing violin. A mutual friend introduced us, and I was soon smitten by her beauty and charm.

It would be several years later, and following one tour in Vietnam, before I would be ready to settle down.

In the summer of 1972, we were married (despite Mary's mother's disapproval) and, over time, came to reside with our three children in Central Minnesota, where the Messages from Heaven would be recorded.

For all of her childhood and adult life, Mary experienced apparitions from the Blessed Mother, Our Lord, Heavenly angels and saints, and even deceased family members. But they were solely personal experiences for members of the family or an occasional close friend. And they were not written down.

Then, in early 1993, the Lord asked Mary to write down her mystical experiences. She did not know why or for what purpose, but she obeyed. Little did we know just how profound those messages would become.

In February of 1993, during a prayer meeting at our parish, the Lord asked Mary to vocalize a message publicly for the very first time, in response to someone there who wanted to be healed. It was not long after, that Our Lord asked us to approach our bishop about the Messages.

At the time, our pastor did not want us going public with the Messages, so out of obedience we continued to keep them private, while keeping our bishop informed as things progressed. Through the bishop's office, we were also directed to a spiritual director, and we continue to see one to this day. Mary also underwent extensive medical and psychological evaluation to ensure that her apparitions were truly beyond the knowledge and explanation of science.

Whenever Mary was to receive a message, be she at home, work, school, or elsewhere, she would promptly excuse herself for the time being, go and receive the message, then return to what she was previously doing, many times with no one the wiser. It never interfered with family life. Even if she were in the middle of a message and was interrupted by a crying child, God the Father would say, "Go, your family needs you," and finish the message with her at a later time.

Some might wonder how we continued to function as a normal family with something so unusual going on in private. In our opinion, the kind of intimacy we have with Our Lord is the same kind of intimacy He longs to have with all of us. If only people knew the great benefits that await us when we trust in the Lord

Introduction

God, Healer and Friend, to care for us, letting Him guide us to when we need care of any kind.

Since Mary did not know, at the time, what God's plan was with these Messages, she did not give much attention, when recording, to what might have been going on in our family, in world news, etc.

Though we do not believe this takes away anything from the Messages, you may be curious at times as to what else may have been going on. Unfortunately, as we were not directed by the Lord to publish these until 2016, we have only what was documented by Mary at the time these were recorded. We have worked very closely with our daughter, the editor, to ensure the integrity of the Messages are kept intact.

The path with God has certainly been interesting. His Way with Mary, though not always easy, has been a very peaceful one. Mary wrote, and continues to write, all the messages long-hand, despite technological advancements.

Heaven has never forced her to write, nor caused her hand to move without her consent. Heaven (God the Father, His Son Jesus, and the Holy Spirit, and any of the saints) only ever makes requests of us, never demands, to record and file these Messages.

So now, may you come to know of Our Lord's great Love for you, as priests. May you enjoy, what we believe to be, some of the most profound and meaningful messages from Our God. And may you realize, just as we did, how much the Lord has walked with you since the moment you were conceived, and how a great and loving Savior holds you in the palm of His Hands through all your joys, all your sorrows, all your ways.

In His Service,

Gregory Kuhn

Note from the Scribe

God is the true author of these books called *Messages from Heaven: For My People*; *Messages from Heaven: For My Priests*. He asked me in 1993 to be His scribe and write down the Messages from Heaven as He would say them to me. I said yes and have felt so blessed to be able to do this for Him.

I grew in knowledge of Him as I listened to His Voice, or heard Our Blessed Mother's Voice, and then the Saints, each one having their own personality. Some have a great sense of humor, and some, like me, speak more seriously and emotionally because of their Mission from God.

Am I the only one to be asked to do this? God has quite obviously used several individuals at various times and places to accomplish His will for the benefit of the human race of which He created with great love. This is my calling at this time, to draw more souls closer to the Lord. Each of us has been asked to do things for God.

Note from the Scribe

May these Messages from Heaven touch your heart to be drawn to serve the Lord.

In His service,

Mary Kuhn

1993 - 1994

November 9, 1993
Our Lord

"I now am calling you, Fr. ***, Bishop ***, and others to rededicate their lives to saving of souls full-time. Leave the Parish worries of money, time, budgets and other earthly worries to others and be about My Father's Plan. To save as many souls as possible. To preach repentance now, to be open to Sacraments being given, especially Reconciliation more often. To be open to their people's needs of their souls. To spend time and energies working totally for Me. To give up earthly concerns and give 100% to preaching the Gospel, to prayer in front of the Blessed Sacrament. I am calling all of you to a special Sainthood. There is not time anymore for extra worries about parish housing or what cars to drive, or future worries about insurance, or retirement.

I beg of you, My Priests, to stop now and prostrate yourselves before the Blessed Sacrament and pray, pray. Pray for not only your own soul but the souls of your parishioners. Do not worry about money or church building upkeep or the latest for the Rectory. Please, I beg of you before it is too late to give Me your all. Your energies, your mind, but mostly your heart. When you give Me your Heart, you gain peace and joy that no one can take from you. I am there for you. I have always been there for you. Be alert to Me and My Promptings in your hearts. Be alert to My Love, My Compassion. Be alert to the suffering souls I bring your way and you will be happiest. I can only ask you to work with Me. I now am asking all My Priests to give their lives back to Me.

If you are afraid, tell Me. If you are angry, tell Me. If you need a hug, tell Me. I am to be there for you and I AM THERE FOR YOU. I AM WITH YOU. I AM HOLDING YOU CLOSE TO MY HEART. I AM THE LORD. I WILL NOT ABANDON YOU.

Let us talk for a moment about abandonment. Have you ever been abandoned? Have you felt such loneliness that you cried? Have you felt such anger at others that you cried? Have you ever felt so much pain that your heart was bursting and you knew not where to go? I have felt this many times. I am your Lord and Savior and I have felt this many times. I have been abandoned by My People. I have been abandoned by the very people I created to love and honor Me. I have been abandoned. I can hardly speak of this as My Heart is in such pain. You can help alleviate some of this pain. You can give back your heart to Me. I will take it and put your heart with My Heart and together We can touch souls. Together We can bring souls to the Lord. Together We can move mountains. Together, together miracles can be worked and souls can be saved. Will you accept this call? Will you come back to Me, your Lord and Savior?"

November 16, 1993

A vision at the Consecration during Mass: I saw Our Lord as the priest and holding the Body of Christ [consecrated bread], and I saw the red on His hands of the Stigmata [wounds of Christ].

Our Lord

"All My Priests suffer the Crucifixion, My Calvary, with Me at each Mass. They are My sign to My People of Redemption. Their hands are blessed at each Mass. They are given special graces to be Me to their People."

Then, as Father genuflected after the Consecration, Our Lord said, in a very proud possessive voice:

"My Priest, My Son, Whom I love so dearly."

November 28, 1993
Our Lord

"When a Priest is mine and is trying very hard to remain holy amidst the worldly demands as a Pastor, I am there, extra duty for him. My Mother has wrapped Her Mantle over him to protect him. When My Mother wraps Her Mantle over someone believe it, they are very protected from harm. Holiness does not come from ease in life, it comes from cross upon cross being offered up for the Glory of God.

My Priests, the holy ones who are trying to remain close to Me, will have special crosses to bear for Me, but I will be there for them to comfort them.

February 14, 1994
Our Lord

"I wish for you to write this evening, a Message to My Beloved Priests. My Heart is open wide to them, for them. I AM knocking constantly at the door of their heart to join My Heart. Together, we can do great things. Together, we Can spread My Love and My Compassion to others.

My Beloved Priests, I wait for you. I, Your Lord and Savior, wait for you. Can you spare one moment in your busy day for Me? Do you remember what I represent, your Salvation. I REPRESENT YOUR SALVATION. Think for a moment what that means, to you, to others. YOU CANNOT ENTER HEAVEN WITHOUT ME. There it is, in simple language. You cannot enter Heaven without Me.

Where are you going? What is your main goal as My Servant, My Priest? What is so important to your success that you risk losing your soul for it? WHAT IS TAKING MY PLACE IN YOUR HEART. I want to know, what could be so important as to take My place, when you will need Me to gain eternal happiness.

I need each of you. I love each of you. Give Me your heart and together we can do great things."

March 5, 1994
Our Lord

"I need My Priests who read this, and other Messages from Me, to rise up and begin a fasting and penance time in their parishes. I NEED THEM TO RISE UP AND PRAY FOR THE SALVATION OF NOT ONLY THEIR SOULS BUT THE SOULS OF OTH-

ERS. IT IS NOT TOO LATE TO BEGIN TO REALIZE THE SERIOUSNESS OF THE WORLD SITUATION. BEGIN NOW TO PRAY IN FRONT OF THE BLESSED SACRAMENT. UNLOCK YOUR CHURCHES AND LET PEOPLE IN TO PRAY. What good will saving the statues and other physical articles in the church be when the souls of My People are being wasted and lost because they have not heard about the state of their souls. Do they know there is Purgatory and Hell? Do they know the Priest is Me to them? Not an administrator of the parish property, not a caretaker of the parish funds, not an organizer of the parish functions, but **FIRST** A PRIEST WHO KNOWS HIS LORD AND IS OPEN DAY AND NIGHT TO HIS PEOPLE. They can approach him night and day to discuss problems of the soul. They can find him holding Confessions, saying Mass, praying in front of the Blessed Sacrament or visiting them in their homes.

They can find Me when they need Me because My Priests are called to be Me at all times, day or night. I have called and given them gifted lay people to take away the burdens of organization and burdens of details of administration so they, My Beloved Priests, can be free to be Me to their people.

I am a saddened Lord when I speak of these things. I shed tears of frustration, of compassion, of love for each of My Priests. The world has dictated other things to you, My Priests, and you have listened to the world. What do you want Me to say to you when you come before Me in Heaven. The gates will not be open yet and what will you want Me to say to you? I CAN ONLY ALLOW THOSE WHO HAVE WALKED WITH ME, WORKED WITH ME, PRAYED WITH ME TO ENTER MY HOME.

You are asking how you can change things when all is going as it is? I AM CHANGE. I AM COMPASSION. I AM HE WHO CREATED THE WORLD. I AM HE WHO CREATED YOU, EACH OF YOU FOR A REASON. THERE IS A PLAN FOR YOU. THERE IS

A PLACE FOR YOU IN HEAVEN. Will it remain empty for eternity? Do you not want to be with Me, for all eternity? The Choice is yours to make as to where you want to go for eternity. I CHOSE YOU FOR A REASON. I NEED YOU TO BE WHAT I CREATED YOU TO BE, ME TO OTHERS.

When you are Me, all of the time to others, you will have the courage, the strength, to throw away the things of the earthly world and take up the virtues of poverty, patience, compassion, love of neighbor, and your heart will be with My Heart. We are united as one at Mass every day. I have a mission for you to do and in these end times, that mission needs to be fulfilled by each of you. People's souls are at stake, and a great deal of responsibility lies with you, My Priests. You can do all of this because I am with you, holding you up and giving you strength when you need it. You are not alone because I will send you others who share in this mission with you. You will have the support you need to continue on in your work.

Give over the parish responsibilities to lay people who will be given to you and spend your time for My People and the salvation of their souls."

August 8, 1994
Our Lord

"My Priests, My Priests, why do you not answer Me. I have created you. I have called you to this vocation. Why do you turn away My Prophets and continue to feel that you have suffered enough? I was crucified that you might live and have My Life within you. I was crucified that you might live and have life more abundantly. I was crucified that you might gain eternal life.

For My Priests

Where are you going? Why do you need more study, more time spent being popular? Where are your priorities? I have come that you may have life and have it more abundantly. BUT NOT THE LIFE OF THE WORLD BUT THE LIFE THAT I YOUR LORD AND SAVIOR CAN GIVE YOU. DO NOT EVER REJECT THIS GIFT OF LIFE. YOU WILL NOT GAIN ETERNAL LIFE.

I Am Your Lord and Savior. I bore you so that you could be Me to the world. I did not call you to be popular as the world defines it, or memorable as the world wants to remember you. I CREATED YOU TO BE ME AND YOU ARE NOT BEING ME BY REJECTING MY MOTHER. YOU ARE NOT BEING ME BY LIVING IN THE WORLD AND OF THE WORLD IN RECTORY BUILDINGS THAT ARE MADE FOR A KING WHILE YOUR OWN FLOCK GO HUNGRY AND LIVE IN HOMES WITH GREAT WANT.

My Priests, My Beloved Priests, when will you stop the fast lane type of life and pray with Me from your heart. When will you throw yourselves at My feet and beg forgiveness and pray for your soul and the souls of your flock of which you are to be the Shepherd. My Priests, My Priests, I cry for the wants of My People. I cry for the needs of My People. Where can they go if they do not see Me in you? Where will they find Me?

Cast away from Me, you hypocrites, and lie in your perversion and hatred, anger and lust. Yes, you who think you are holy must be servants to others. SERVANTS, I said to you, and you look at Me as if you do not know its meaning. Give, My Priests, until it hurts in your body and heart. Give, give to My People before it is too late. The time as you know it is very slim for mankind to save themselves.

We, in Heaven, are now searching for the souls who will listen with the piece of their heart that is still dedicated to Me, their Lord and Savior. We, in Heaven, are relying on each of you who reads this Message, each of you who hears this Message, to go to My Home, in front of the Blessed Sacrament, and ask My forgiveness for your slow response to My Call. Ask also for the graces to continue with this Ministry. I HAVE CALLED YOU, ALL OF YOU, TO [THE] SPIRIT OF THE LORD MINISTRY. *(This means total dedication to our Lord Jesus Christ.)* Do not question what, or why, or how come, to this person these Messages were given. I will work with certain servants of mine and they are responsible for what I want them to do.

You are responsible for what I want you to do. Come together for weekly meetings of prayer in front of the Blessed Sacrament. Open these prayer times up to all your people, to anyone who wishes to come or to those whom I send. DO NOT, I repeat, do not expect to hire speakers and have refreshments. THIS IS A VERY, VERY, SERIOUS TIME OF PRAYER for all My People. Your personal salvation depends on this prayer time in front of the Blessed Sacrament.

For those who are questioning how this can be fitted into your busy schedules. I SAY TO YOU WHERE DO I FIT IN YOUR LIFE. I, THE LORD OF THE UNIVERSE. I, THE CREATOR OF THE WORLD. WHAT DOES IT TAKE FOR YOU TO UNDERSTAND THAT I HAVE CHOSEN YOU. I LOVE, LOVE, LOVE YOU BEYOND DESCRIPTION. I WANT YOU TO BE WITH ME AND MY MOTHER AND ALL THE SAINTS.

Lean on My prophets, and I will answer your questions. Lean on Me, and I will comfort you and save you from yourselves and your worldly cravings. Do not hesitate one second. Work in these prayer times before and after your Masses. Hold one night a week for family prayer. Bring My little children to Me to spend a few minutes in talking to Me. YOU DO NOT NEED ALL THE TRAPPINGS OF MUSIC, NOISE FROM THE PEOPLE WHO TALK LOUDLY IN MY HOME. Keep reverence in church.

For My Priests

Let My People come to Me as they are poor, wealthy, angry, peaceful, searching souls that I, their Lord and Savior, can help to find the peace, joy, and love that only I can give them.

My Priests, please listen and give Me your answer of yes, and do it now. Come together, and proclaim the greatness of the Lord. Throw away your fears of lay people and their power. Throw away your fears of loss of power and material possessions. I AM ALL YOU NEED.

Open up your Confessionals, and stay there until all of My People have had an opportunity to confess their sins so I, their personal Lord and Savior, can forgive them.

Your heart needs to be in the right place. You cannot do My work if you are full of anger and resentment, or you feel you would rather have the world.

Give Me your all, and you will receive graces and will be able to endure the crosses that will come your way, because you said yes to Me.
My Priests, I have given you this Message. You must go forward now and begin all that I have asked for in all of these Messages. I need you to begin work, and to DO IT NOW.

Instantly, I can hear the response of your heart saying, 'He gave many messages that said "now" in the Bible, and the events happened centuries later.' I ASK YOU TO DO IT NOW. This moment that you read this.

If you are a Bishop, these Messages and all the Messages are for your Diocese. If you are a Priest of a Parish, these Messages are for your Parish. If you are a Deacon, then you will work with the Pastor of your Parish to do these things I am asking of you.

If you are a Married Couple reading this, then you will be together in unity with My Heart in sharing these Messages with each other and your family. If you are a Single Person, you will be desperately needed to gather souls for Me and will feel you will want to share these with your Friends and others.

If you are growing Children and you have just begun to learn about Me, then you will find peace and love that only I can give.

If you have given your life to Me as a Nun in a Community, then your community will need to be given these Messages, and you will want to share with all whom you know and meet.

I have asked certain People to come forward and receive from Me a special anointing. They know who they are. They will be very busy now proclaiming these Messages to those who need to hear them and see them."

August 23, 1994
Our Lord

"I am calling on you again to pray earnestly for My People. They do not know the horrible abyss they will be going to if they do not repent and follow Me, their Lord and Savior.

I am saddened by what I see and hear. My Heart is ripped open wider by My Priests who do not repent and change their lives. I have called each of them to the Priesthood for a reason.

I need each of them desperately to come forward and acknowledge that they know Me and they will listen to Me. There are so few who have abandoned themselves to Me. They comfort Me with their prayers, their desires to be the complete Priest I want them to be. I am a just God. I will remember those who remembered Me. I will deal with each soul according to what they have done with their Vocation.

I cannot begin to tell you of the joy My Mother has when each soul gives Me their all. She has been working for Centuries to give Her all to the Redemption of the world. If only the world would listen to Her and My Prophets that I continue to send to warn My People."

September 5, 1994
Our Lord

"Now, you are wondering how all of these Priests fit into The Plan. I have asked each of those that you have met to abandon themselves to Me and to go forward without fear, without hesitation, to follow the Messages given to them as Priests. I have been somewhat disappointed in their responses. Yes, they want to move slowly, yes, they are afraid, yes, some of this will take time. But I SAY TO THEM, THERE IS NO TIME. IT IS NOW, THE TIME TO ACT IS NOW. THERE CAN NO LONGER BE HESITATION. THERE CAN NO LONGER BE FEAR. STEP OUT IN FAITH, STEP OUT IN FAITH, STEP OUT WITH JOY BECAUSE THIS WILL BE YOUR SALVATION. Your lives are hanging on a thread of hope, will you make it to the Promised Land? Not without Prayer, NOT WITHOUT FOLLOWING THE MESSAGES. NOW, NOW, NOW, do not sit in your homes, your Rectories, your palaces that you have been given. Leave them and go out to My People.

If I stated in the Messages to fast and do penance as a Parish, or as a People, or as a Priest, THEN WHY DO I NOT SEE YOU DOING IT? Do not, I repeat, do not accept these answers My Servant, from anyone, such as:

1. This is something that takes time.

2. All of these Messages must be studied and put into a long red-tape process.

3. We can't move yet on this because we have to discuss what's happening here.

4. I don't know what else to do, I have done all of these things asked for in the Messages.

Woe unto you who have taken lightly what My Prophets say."

September 20, 1994
Our Lord

"I am disappointed in My Priests. The Priests I created and carried through their lifetimes. These Priests are causing pain to My Heart, My Sacred Heart. Why do I bother to ask them? Why do I not look elsewhere? Why must this continue, this degradation to My People from My People.

I am a saddened God. Where will I be able to find servants willing to comfort Me, willing to comfort their brother. Why must My Father continue the world as it is when He could annihilate the world now. Where are My Servants?

I call, night and day, but they turn away. I ask them over and over, and they walk away. They, My People, walk away. They, My People, scoff at Me and say, 'There's a better way. I'm on my way, I'm on my way to a better world, the world's way. Don't bother me, I can do it myself. I don't need you anymore. I don't need you anymore.'

My Heart aches, My People, what have I done to create such monsters I see before Me. Where is your heart? Where are you the lovable, cuddly baby, the eager young child, the frustrated teenager, the challenged adult? Where in you can I find the heart I created? The heart filled with compassion and love. Show Me, your Lord and Savior, where is your heart? Where is the heart filled with love and compassion?

Jesus,
the Sorrowing Heart"

October 16, 1994
Our Lord

"I am saddened this evening for My Priests. They are running here and there and need to take more time for quiet time with Me. It is very hard to do in this world, and satan uses 'busyness' as a reason for success. People no longer have time for Church and time for each other. I am saddened because I have given My People so much. They have all the tools they need for a good life, yet they desire to walk the way of the world.

Woe be to them who walk with satan. They will find it very, very, difficult to come into My Home, Heaven. Pray for them, as they need all prayers for their salvation. I will speak with you later.

I remain your intimate friend,
Jesus"

November 28, 1994
Our Lord

"The Priests who I call to this Vocation have given Me their heart long ago. When they say yes to the Priesthood, it is a huge step.

They learn how to counsel People, how to be close to their parishioners, how to run a Parish successfully. They need so much positive feedback because theirs is a thankless Vocation, humanly speaking. They are in the public eye but constantly scrutinized how they speak, how they act, how they dress. They are no longer themselves, most of them, but a product of what their parishioners wish them to be. Most have given themselves over to the world and its allurements including women. Some have gone as far as giving up the Priesthood completely in order to feel that peace and joy they had at one time with Me, when they started their Vocation.

Now you are seeing a little part of what I desire you to see. Bring My Priests back to Me. Do not let them become filled with the world and its temptations. BRING THEM BACK TO ME."

December 2, 1994
Our Lord

"I need to speak to My Priests. I need to have them know how much I love them. I want them to know how much I need them. I want them to know how each one is important to Me, their Lord and Savior.

My beloved Priests, of whom I place My Church and its People. My Beloved Priests, whom I cherish and watch over and protect. I, your Lord and Savior, speak to you now on the subject of Daily Masses. Take time to say My Mass every day. Do not let any one day go by that you have missed doing the most important devotion a Priest can do for His Lord and Savior, with His Lord and Savior, to speak. Adore, and pray My Mass, My Remembrance to My People, My gift to you and to them. Do you not believe that I AM HE THAT CAME TO TAKE AWAY YOUR SINS? Do you not believe that I AM HE THAT DIED FOR YOU

SO YOU COULD BE SAVED? Do you not believe that the Sacrifice of the Mass is truly Me, again and again, dying for you, again and again, suffering for you that you might have life and have it more abundantly? Do you not believe that you as a Priest, are specifically called to hold Me in your hands, to lift Me up to My People, to invite My People to come back to me, to beg My People to partake in Me, the REAL JESUS, THE ALIVE JESUS, THE JESUS THAT IS YOURS AND THEIR SALVATION?

It is truly Me, your Lord and Savior, at the Mass, dying again for His People. I AM HE. I AM THE ONE SENT BY GOD TO BE SAVIOR OF THE WORLD. BELIEVE IT. IT IS SO, AS WRITTEN.

My Beloved Priests, do not, I beg of you, from My deepest parts of My Heart, do not let an opportunity pass you by that you could offer the Sacrifice of My Mass to My People. Do not let it pass by you, for your salvation rests on this, that you do your duties as My Priest, to My People, before you do the duties assigned by the world.

I am a jealous God. I want My Priests totally dedicated to Me, and to no one else. I Repeat, I want My Priests totally dedicated to Me, their Lord and Savior, and to no one else."

December 9, 1994
Our Lord

"Where are you, My servant, My Beloved Priest? Where are you going in such a hurry? I need you to come back to Me, your Lord and Savior. Come back to the basics of your Priesthood. Come back to be with Me.

I have felt such sadness from your heart. Did I not create you and bring you into this world to work for Me, your Lord and

Savior? Did I not give you everything you need? Did I not hold you when you were sick, comfort you when you were sad, love you no matter where you were at? Come back to Me, My beloved Priest, and love Me. Love Me. Do not be afraid to bolt out into My world of love and compassion. There is nothing I would not do for you. There is nothing I would not give you. Listen to Me and follow My Plan for you. I have called you to the Priesthood. I have called you to live the life of chastity, obedience, and love to My People. As a Priest, you are filled with a special grace from Me, your Lord and Savior. I have not abandoned you. I have been here for you, loving you.

Do not delay. Pray before the Blessed Sacrament. I have forgiven you and desire you to continue on the path of holiness as a Priest. I need you to be 100% dedicated to Me and not to have worries about the world and its desires.

My People need holy Priests. Priests filled with dedication to their calling. Do not delay but come back to Me, and I will comfort you. You are in the Parish I desire you to be in. You are in the Community I desire you to be in. You are in the Diocese I desire you to be in. I can take care of all your worries and cares for you. I am your personal Lord and personal Savior.

I love you. I will never abandon you. You are mine. My own.

Your personal Friend,
Jesus"

December 1994
Our Lord

I asked the Lord, "What are the Priests to do if they already are doing what is spoken of in the Messages?"

Our Lord answered with a vision:

I could see as if in a moving video: Masses of Healing, special educational Missions given one week here, another week at various Catholic Churches but using the expertise of Priests and with specially trained Lay People for the adult catechesis.

The big feeling I was given was of unity between the Priests and their Bishop, and working together to help build up each other, plus parishes and congregations.

The feeling of peace and joy pervaded the scenes. Education of the people was of great importance: Why are they Catholic, what are they doing, and where is their emphasis in life?

December 18, 1994
Our Lord

"I am concerned that you pray for My Priests, as each of them has their own crucifixion to go through. Each has to answer to Me, their Lord and Savior. Each has to give up the worldly temptations and go with Me into a world of penance and sacrifice. Sometimes these worlds get mixed up for them and they find themselves floundering, looking for their direction again."

1995 - 1998

January 18, 1995
Our Lord

"I need you to pray for the graces to combat the evil that is in our world and for the Healing Masses to begin soon. My Priests need to come together, and I am disappointed that it is taking so long. They have heard My Word, but they do not listen. The world has them corralled into thinking they are very important and to keep their schedules filled with all sorts of business. They need to pray more and to be comforted in My Presence.

Oh, how My Heart aches for the sorrows of My People. So many are wandering lost in the crowd.

Continue on, oh good and faithful servants. In this way you bring peace and joy to My Suffering Heart and the Suffering Heart of My Mother.

Jesus,

Your friend, through to eternity and beyond"

January 30, 1995
Our Lord

"Do not worry that you are not doing enough for Me, your Lord and Savior. I see your frustration. I see your anger with Priests not answering My Call.

Pray for My Beloved Priests. They need so much love and prayers. They are very tired and mixed up on ideas and are questioning where is the Church going.... They have been crucified with Me so many times. Pray, and have compassion for them. I love them and will continue to protect them.

I love you and will continue to protect you. Be happy, be Me to others today; That is what I wish you to do for Me. Be Me. My love until we speak later.

Jesus"

March 1, 1995
Our Lord

"My Priests, My Beloved Priests, are choosing the way of the world. Very, very few of My Chosen ones will desire to walk My Way of the Cross in their life. The world has encouraged them to become rude, selfish, arrogant persons who play the role of the Priest but do not practice the Love of their Lord or the true love of their neighbor. They are on a popularity contest with one another, and My Calling them from this they cannot accept.

If My Priests would be what they are to be, My Sign of Love and Compassion to My People, then the Messages would already be made public, you could be doing more of what I desire you to do for My People, and many souls could be saved.

Yes, I am Lord, and Yes, I will deliver a sign, but I say to My Priests, 'YOU ARE THE SIGN.' You have My Mass, My personal Way of the Cross with the Consecration of My Body and My Blood, the offering of Myself to My People so their sins will be forgiven. I will come again to save My People, but only a few will be ready.

I say to you, My Beloved Priests, how can you prepare My People for the awesome moment of judgement day, when you yourselves have not prepared for your own death. Woe to you who have knowledge of these things and do not teach this to My People.

Yes, you preach of love of neighbor and love of God. Do you preach repentance, and do you describe the horrors of what is to come if My People do not repent? Do you beg them to be on their knees in asking for forgiveness? Do you leave the soft touch, and go and speak from your heart about how I can be a loving and forgiving God but also a just God? I will be judge and jury for My People, and yet days are floating by and time is running out for mankind.

DO NOT SIT IN YOUR RECTORIES AND EXPECT TO BE SAVED BECAUSE YOU ARE A PRIEST. **Expect to be judged on how you dedicated and lived your life.** You have been called to one of the greatest vocations: that of a life being Me to others. The intimacy we share at the Mass, My Supreme Sacrifice, cannot be duplicated to anyone else in any other vocation. You have been called. I chose each of you for this Vocation. DO NOT SHRUG OFF YOUR DUTIES, YOUR RESPONSIBILITY FOR THE SOULS OF MY PEOPLE. Stay with Me and work with Me, your Lord and Savior."

May 8, 1995
Our Lord

"I, your Lord and Savior, wish to speak to you, each of you, thanking you for supporting Me in your Vocation. My Heart is at rest when I see you holding My Body and My Blood in your hands reverently.

My Heart is at rest when I see you prostrate in prayer before the Blessed Sacrament. My Heart is at rest when I see you comforting My People in the Confessional. My Heart is at rest when I see you feeding the hungry, clothing the naked, and giving shelter to those in need. My Heart is at rest when you visit the sick, the infirmed, the lonely, those in jails and prisons. My Heart is at rest when I see you surrender your life to Me so I may use you as a shining light to My People.

I love you, My Beloved Priests. Stand firm in your Vocation and stay close to Me, your Lord and Savior. I need each of you now as the end times are approaching. You will be My light to My People, My comfort to My Heart. Go now to love and serve with joy, My People.

Jesus"

May 30, 1995
Our Lord

"To My Beloved Priests, how I love you. How I ache for you to remain with Me in prayer in front of the Blessed Sacrament after your daily Masses with me.

Why do you rush to be off to worldly pleasures? You have forgotten how important prayer with Me is. Is this not what your

Vocation is all about? To spend time with your main lover, intimate friend and director of your life?

Where are you going in such a hurry? Why are you not encouraging your People, My People, I have given you to adore their Lord and Savior? Why are you not concerned that My People are losing their love for Me? Could you encourage them to spend time with Me after Mass? Even fifteen minutes spent with Me cannot be measured in the amount of graces earned for that person.

As a Priest, you hold Me every day in your hands as you are the tool I use to work through as the bread and wine are changed into My Body and My Blood. MY BODY AND MY BLOOD. IT IS REAL. THE MIRACLE HAPPENS EVERY MASS, EVERY CONSECRATION. I do not choose to do it with certain Priests or certain congregations or certain parishes. I AM REAL. I AM GOD. WITH ME ANYTHING IS POSSIBLE.

You, My Beloved Priests, you have forgotten what you are called to do, to be Me to My People. If you show reverence and adoration to My Body and My Blood, My People will imitate you. If you rush through the Mass because My People need to rush home and make meals, or its running time-wise too long and criticism will come your way...

My Priests, My Priests, you have looked to your People for consolation instead of to Me. I need to have your undivided attention. You work for Me, not under the direction of My People. Yes, you are to be obedient to your Pope. Yes, you are to be obedient to your Bishop. Be careful that the obedience you listen to are the rules set up by Me, your Lord and Savior and Creator of the World and not a human being who is looking for power.

Be careful, My Beloved Priests that what My People see in you is the love and compassion portrayed in the Gospels. Be careful that your heart has not strayed into foreign territory where it does not belong.

Come back to Me, your Lord and your personal Savior. Strip yourselves of your worldly belongings in your heart and surrender to Me as you did when I chose you personally by name to be My Priest in the Order of Melchizedek, to have and to hold from that day forward a new covenant with Me in your heart. You joined your heart with My Heart. I have not changed or moved. I know you, I created you. I love you.

Spend time with Me in prayer in the front of the Blessed Sacrament. Love Me, as you desire to love Me. I am there for you. I need you to be Me to My People. Stay with Me, My Beloved Priests, and do not shirk your duties as My Servants.

Jesus"

June 9, 1995
Our Lord

"My Mother desires very much that these Messages get to My People. The Priests' souls, the souls of My People, that will be saved because of these Messages, that is what you must remember; it is the Messages that are important, not Greg and Mary Kuhn, or other People mentioned in them. Keep this in mind Fr. *** that the Messenger is not important here. MY MESSAGES ARE VERY IMPORTANT. THEY TELL MY PEOPLE TO COME BACK TO ME BEFORE IT IS TOO LATE FOR THEM. Believe Me, even as we speak there are souls losing eternal life, many souls never given the chance to repent. *[They did not prepare well for their death.]*

Listen and follow Me as I asked My Apostles to do. Listen and follow Me; your reward will be great in Heaven. I will take care of all of your worldly worries and cares. I love all of you enough that I will protect you and watch over you so *no harm shall come to you, no arrow strike you down.* You have My Word, as your Lord and Savior. I will protect you all from the terrors of satan and the reverberations of rejection you will feel at times because you have said yes to Me.

Come now, and pray together with Me the Our Father, Hail Mary, Glory Be to the Father. Be with Me as I listen to you and you listen to Me.

Your intimate friend always,
Jesus"

June 9, 1995
Our Lord

"Offer up your pain of heart, mind, and head today *[Mary]* for your Confessor and others who have a great deal of surrendering to do to trust God fully. It is so much easier to look at life from the trained Priestly point of view, the Gospels daily, and the gift of The Eucharist.

My Priests become spoiled with My Presence, My Closeness to them. I become ordinary and common place to them. If I manifest Myself to anyone who is hurting from drug addiction or chemical despondency, or other afflictions, they deal with those easily as the person is hurting and programs of healing are in place both humanly and Divine.

However, when I manifest Myself to you *[Mary]* as I have been with Greg, your family, friends and others, very much aware that this is different, they *[My Ordained]* cannot see all I am doing. They cannot see all I plan to do. They cannot see a program built in to work here, a Program that has been used before. A Program that is definable and easily laid out in their educated minds.

Yes, My People have grown accustomed to Programs for this and that ailment. What about programs for the Heart? They have those too. These programs use the well run, well planned programs that deal with healing and prayer groups and egotistical settings of one blessed person or gifted to other non-gifted people.

Where am I their Lord, their Creator in all of this? Where do I belong in the mainstream of their life? In their prayer group? Oh, Yes, they know where I AM, truly.

December 16, 1995
Our Lord

On this particular weekend, our new bishop was visiting our parish priest, and I was wanting to give him a special honor. This was Our Lord's response to His priests:

"I AM THE MASS. ANYONE WHO ATTENDS THE MASS IS NOT TO BE PUT IN MY PLACE OF HONOR. I AM HE. I AM WHO AM.

Do not pretend that this does not mean anything to you. You are called to be Me, to sing the Mass as I assist you. That is your Ministry. I AM ALIVE. I AM WHO AM. Do not desecrate what I have consecrated and made Holy in My Name.

Do you love Me? I love you, all of you, as you are, as you try to be, as you desire to be. LOVE ME, all of you; please love Me, your Lord and Savior, Jesus Christ.

Will you give up the world for Me? I am asking again, because I need you to give up all the glitter, excitement, money that goes into this season and envelop yourself in prayer with Me, your delightful Savior. I need to be intimate with you. I desire to be intimate and to share My intimate self with you.

Listen to the Angels singing. It is the time of rejoicing."

October 29, 1996
Our Lord

"My Beloved Priests, do not stay so far from Me. I have not deserted you. I AM TRULY WITH YOU. I have not forgotten you. You have a special place in My Heart. Is that not how it should be for ones so anointed by Me to represent Me to My People? Is this not love? Is this not My Loving You?

To each of you, I have asked to be crucified with Me. To each of you I have asked you to be Me to My People when they have scoffed at you, ridiculed you and called you many vile names. Did I not also suffer as you are suffering? May I share this suffering with you, asking of you only that you talk to Me, permit Me to be an important part of your life?

Come then, and let Us go together to the Mountain to pray, for in this you will find My Presence. In this will be My Love, My Peace, My Joy that will clothe you completely, so you will know I AM YOU and YOU ARE ME and together Our Hearts will conquer the world of sin.

Together, We shall go forth to spread My Gospel, to love My People, to save as many souls as We can save. Come then, My Beloved Priests, to the Mountain with Me, away from your heavy burdens of worldly cares. Come then to Me, your personal Lord and Savior. My Heart is waiting for your heart.
Come, for you will not be disappointed. I love you, as no other can love you. I chose you to be My Priest for My People. Come then, and let us celebrate together this great union. I wait for you. I call your name. Come and be with Me. I, too, feel alone and abandoned. I, too, feel such sorrow that I feel My Heart has been broken in many places. Come then, let Us share together this great love."

December 12, 1996
Our Lord, to His Priests, to His People

"Come, My Servants, and be with Me as I ask this of you: pray for My Church. The foundation has been dangerously uprooted. There are many who are questioning My existence. There are many who do not believe I AM WHO AM. There are many who cannot stand to see Me get any credit, any honor, any respect for THEY FEEL THEY KNOW ALL THE ANSWERS TO ALL THE PROBLEMS. PRIDE is the sin that takes many to the abyss of Hell.

This is My cry to you, help replace these idols of the world with Me. Assist My People to come back to Me. I AM REAL. I AM THE TRUE GOD. I AM THE ONE THEY LOOK AT IN THE TABERNACLES OF THEIR CHURCHES. I AM THE ONE WHO HEARS THEM AND SEES THEM. I AM REAL. THERE IS NO REPLACEMENT FOR ME. THEY RECEIVE ALL OF ME WHEN THEY RECEIVE MY BODY, MY BLOOD in the act of receiving Communion. The Adoration of My Body, My Blood, in Holy

For My Priests

Communion My People have forgotten. I am ridiculed, walked on, stared at, scoffed at. It is a repeat of My Way of the Cross.

My Beloved Priests, whom I created to carry Me, hold Me, caress Me at every Mass. I AM WITH YOU IN PERSON. WHEN YOU HOLD THE HOST AT THE CONSECRATION AND YOU ASK ME TO COME AND CHANGE THE BREAD INTO MY BODY **I AM THERE**. IT IS CONSUMMATED WHEN YOU ASK THAT THE WINE BE CHANGED INTO MY BLOOD **I AM THERE**. IT IS DONE. YOU ARE HOLDING ME. ALL OF ME**. I AM THERE**. You hold Me, caress Me, love Me, and your love for Me transcends to Heaven and then to My People. The love I have for you cannot be wholly comprehended by you. It is so profound. I AM YOUR LORD, Your Personal Savior. THERE IS NO OTHER THAT LOVES YOU AS I DO.

Remember when I asked you to be Me to My People as a Priest in the Order of Melchizedek? I remember. I have not forgotten.

Do not go so far from Me. Let Me hold you, wipe away your tears from your heart and help you to ease the suffering of My People. I ask you not to be afraid of what you see and hear. I have you in the Palm of My Hand where nothing can hurt you. Be at peace. Be Confident. Be open to Me and what I desire you to do for Me. Be open to all I desire to give you.

Do not be afraid to step out in confidence because I say this to you: I AM WITH YOU. I am asking this of you. I need you to be all you can be with My direction. You need not fear for other tasks to get completed. Is it not important that you do as I ask of you? I will take care of all other things for you, your Pastorship, your People, your Family, your Friends.

I love you. In this for you is everything. Come and hold Me now as My Heart is sorrowful. I love you.

Your Jesus,
Lover of your Heart, Spouse to your Soul"

March 13, 1997
Our Lord

"I say to you, My Beloved Priests, take Me as your leader, your master, your beloved. Do not let the world come in and destroy what you have committed to Me, your complete selves. You gave your life over to Me on the moment you committed your life to Me and received the Sacrament of Ordination, graces of which will carry you through your life with Me.

Each of you have been given a journey with Me that only you can walk. All other calls will not give you the peace, love, and joy, that the call to My Priesthood has given you.

Be steadfast in your calling. Be firm in your faith. Be loving to each other and to all My People. Do not hesitate to sacrifice your life as a Priest so My People may live in Me, with Me, and for Me.

I love each of you with an unconditional love. There is nothing I would not do for you. Ask, and it shall be given to you. Seek Me, and you will find Me. Knock, and I will answer you with all the love, peace and joy that only I can give you. Love Me.

Jesus,
your beloved companion"

August 7, 1997
Our Lord

"How I ache for you. My Heart beats in agony for you. I look for your faces to turn toward Me. I yearn for your voices to be raised in supplication to Me. I wait for your call that you need Me. I wait, My Beloved Priests, I wait.

When will you see that all is for the Honor and Glory of God? What I, your Lord, your personal Lord and Savior, have called you to do is be Me to My People, to sacrifice all so that you may be able to be Me at the altar of the Cross – you hold Me, you touch Me, you say words of love and praise to Me, you thank God – but where is your heart? Is it with Me? Where is your heart?

If I called you to Me today, could you say to Me, 'I have done what you have asked of me, Lord?' Could you say that to Me with confidence? Have you said yes to everything I have asked of you? Have you given Me your whole heart, your whole soul, your whole mind? Or is it lost to the attractions of the world and to the evil one who grabs at anyone he can and is allowed to. Have you given Me everything?

What did you say to Me, your Lord, as you accepted My call to you to become a Priest for Me? Do you remember your moment of commitment? I do. I remember all you have said and done. I know all you will do for Me. I ask you again My Priests, My Beloved Priests, to come before Me in the Blessed Sacrament and renew your vows with Me. Come and renew your souls, so I may renew in you an abundance of My peace, My love, My joy. For in Me, you can do anything, as you call upon My Name of Jesus.

Come then, and do not be afraid. I am a merciful God. I am a God of Love. I am a Just God. In Me you will find all you need to be My Priest. Come.

Your Jesus,
Personal friend, companion, lover of My Priests"

May 5, 1998
Our Lord

"You are here with Me. I thank you for your sacrifice. Pray very hard for My Priests. Too many are passing up graces they should be accepting and My promptings they should be listening to.

Pray for My Priests, My Beloved Priests. So many are losing the confidence in Me and in the Sacrament of Holy Orders. So many do not believe in Transubstantiation. So many do not believe in Me. So many, Mary, so many.

Pray for them, that they will have the grace to return to Me and believe. So many, Mary, are in need. I write this as My Heart is breaking for My People. So many have heard but yet do not believe, have seen and yet do not believe. Fear is running rampant over My People's hearts, infiltrating so deeply that even the mention of My Name Jesus brings no spark, but a very faint signal of recognition, a very, very, faint signal.

How will My People find Me? How will they know I AM WHO AM? How will they be alert enough when I call their name to answer Me. Fear has permeated all parts of the world: fear of the unknown, fear of strangers, yet I teach Brotherly Love; fear of confrontation, yet I teach Patience; fear of Love, yet I teach

Chastity and love and respect of your body as the Temple of the Holy Spirit.

Be not afraid, I say to My People, and they answer, 'I must live my life alone, secure as I can make it, relying only on myself because at least I know who I am. I need no one, no one to tell me what to do. I am the person I have to answer to, so leave me alone and never return.'

I look at them with such love, such compassion, and they do not see Me, they do not feel Me, they do not want to know Me. Involvement with Me means sacrifice, hard work, empathy, compassion for the lowly ones, great love of all, patience in all situations, My guiding Hand, My Presence of My Peace, My Love, My Joy. To each person, I have given all they need to succeed in the world I created for them. Everything they are, I gave them. Everything they have, I gave them. Everything they are to be, I have planned for them. Everything they want to be, I will assist them. I LOVE WHAT I HAVE CREATED. YOU ARE MINE. 'I have gifted you,' I say to the soul, and joy overflows, security is with them, and love, My love, which no one can take from them.

How I love My People. How I yearn for their love in return.

Your Beloved Jesus,
Savior of the World"

2005 - 2016

April 3, 2005
Our Lord

I see the needs of My People. I hear their cries of need. I, alone, know who I will Ordain and when. There is not to be man's decision here. A 'yes' is all I need when I call someone to work especially for Me. The souls of My People are special. I call, but man can say no. I call those whom I choose, to represent Me to My People. I CHOOSE; MAN DOES NOT CHOOSE. The call to serve Me is great.

I do not call just anyone. I call the soul that will sacrifice. I call the heart that will be open to Me and will listen to My directives. I call man. Man does not call Me. Man does not 'sign up' for a task. I ORDAIN. I CALL THE SOUL. I CALL SPECIFIC PEOPLE TO DO SPECIFIC TASKS FOR ME. I CALL. I ORDAIN. I AM THE LORD GOD. THERE IS NO OTHER.

Be still, mankind, and listen to your God, your Lord and Savior. You are in territory of the soul. I ALONE AM IN CONTROL OF MAN. I ALONE AM THEIR GOD. NO ONE SHALL EVER BE ME, NO ONE. I AM HE. I CAME THAT ALL MAY HAVE LIFE. THE LIFE I GIVE THEM. I CALL. I ORDAIN. I AM HE. Never forget what your God, your Lord has done for you.

My Heart is saddened. Where are My People? Oh, how I ache for My People. They wander so, searching for some peace, some happiness, and they will not find it if they do not find Me."

September 14, 2006
Our Lord

"My dearest beloved, continue to pray for Fr. ***, and for all My Priests. So many are in great need of Me, so many do not focus on Me, so many are in touch with themselves and the world and so desperately need Me. I AM THERE FOR THEM. They do not listen. I care for them; they do not acknowledge I exist. I love them; they love themselves.

Oh, how My People need Me. Oh, how My Priests need Me and are failing My People. Who will save My People's souls, who?"

September 16, 2006
Our Blessed Mother

"Is there any other way but the Lord's Way? Is there any other Church but the One, True, Church Our Lord Jesus founded, died for, rose again to relieve His People, His Beloved People of the burden of death forever. My dearest daughter of Our Lord Jesus Christ. Is there any other way but the Lord's Way? Come now, let us together extol His Name, Praise Him forever and ever.

Come, let us together give thanks to God for His many Blessings, especially the Blessings of HIS CHURCH, the Blessings of HIMSELF to His People. There is no other way but the Lord's Way."

January 22, 2007
Our Blessed Mother

"My dearest daughter of Our Lord Jesus Christ, Praise the Lord always. He is everything. There is no other. He is the Lord Almighty. Praise His Name forever and ever.

I have called you this early in the morning to ask you today to pray for all Priests, all Priests: those who have died, those who are dying, those who need soul assistance from Us, those who are newly ordained, those who are newly retired, those who have not been obedient, those who have been martyred, those who are working diligently for the Lord, those who are working to be great saints, those who are up for canonization, those who are wandering not knowing their faith; these, Mary, I work so hard for. Help Me with these souls, in a special way, give up something or work on tasks that are laborious so some of these souls will listen today.

Pray, Mary, for My Priests, My Beloved Priests who are in such need, such need. The world doesn't know what to do with Priests; how to treat them, what to give them, how to take care of them. This is truly a crisis in God's Church. My Son sorrows so over the world and its disobedience to Him.

Pray, Mary, for God's People. Where are they going? To where are they rushing? To what are they slaving? To whom is their allegiance?

Pray, Mary, we need you. I will speak later; My Love, and thank you for listening and obeying."

July 9, 2007
Our Lord

"My Heart is saddened. Yes, My People do not listen to My Priests, My dedicated Priests, so in love with Me, so passionate with their call. THIS IS TRULY A VERY SAD DAY FOR ME, your Lord and Savior. I also grieve with you.

My beloved Priests, do not be afraid. I have placed you where I need you. Do not be afraid. I have trained you for this: I AM WITH YOU, always with you, holding you, carrying you, YOU ARE MINE. I AM YOURS. Do not be afraid.

My Guidance to you: follow your heart, your heart attached to the Eucharist, your heart in My Heart.

Follow explicitly the laws of My Church. Follow explicitly the Complete Sacrifice of the Mass. Follow explicitly all you have been taught, by Me, for the souls of My People. Do not be afraid, I am with you for all of your days. I am with you through everything.

You are to be Me to My People. My Beloved People who wander so yearning for Me, yearning for Me. This is My explicit directive to you: go and be Me to My People. Do not be afraid. You know Me for you are Me to My People.

Go now, and be Me to My People. This is My Command of love to you. I will speak again later, always My love is with you.

Jesus,
Savior of the World, King of Heaven and Earth.
I AM WHO AM. There is no other."

July 12, 2007
Our Blessed Mother

"My dearest daughter of Our Lord Jesus Christ, thank you for obeying Our Lord. There is very much more to come. They will need you to be there with them, as God's Messenger for the now-time of their life. Yes, they have Isaiah, they have many Prophets to turn to, but Our Lord wishes for you to be His spokesperson to His Beloved Priests.

How He loves them. They have surrendered over everything to Him, everything. He, in turn, desires, if allowed by them, to give them everything. He will provide all for them, they need only to surrender all to Him.

Yes, there will always be those who will request, demand, invite chaos because there will always be the struggle for God's People between good and evil. The choices they make are not always the wisest.

God sends His Priests to assist His People to know Him, to love Him, to serve Him. In this is their salvation, for they bring The Eucharist to His People, the Christ they so need, want, and cannot live without.

This, then, is the best gift to the world for mankind: HIS PRIESTS.

Let us pray then, Mary, with a greater effort for Priests, all of God's Priests.

I know you need rest. Go now to rest, we will speak later.

My love as Your Mother,
Queen of Heaven and Earth."

September 17, 2007
Our Lord

Jesus has come now in His Vestments as King of Heaven and Earth, very bright, majestic, profoundly Holy, profoundly Holy. He is now saying:

"My dear Priests, My givers of love to the souls of My People. I AM HE. THERE IS NO OTHER. BELIEVE, IT IS TRULY ME. I AM HE. THERE IS NO OTHER.

My dear Priests, so close to My Heart, do not be afraid. I say again, do not be afraid. All will be for the Greater Honor and Glory of God. ALL WILL BE FOR THE GREATER HONOR AND GLORY OF GOD.

You are troubled by My People's questions, to their insistence that they are right, they are to be listened to.

I say to you, as your Lord and Savior, I say to you, My Priests, My Beloved Priests, so close to My Heart, do not be afraid. I have given you all you need to work with My People. I have given you all you need to work with My People.

I say to you again. DO NOT BE AFRAID. Go out to all the world and tell the Good News. I AM HE. THERE IS NO OTHER.

Be patient, yes, be loving, yes, but never be afraid. You have Me, you have Me, you hold Me, you live Me, you love Me. Is there any other way to live, but with Me? Is there any other life, but with Me? Then I say to you again, do not be afraid.

Come to Me, day and night, and give to Me all your problems, all your cares, your worries. I know what to do with them. I care for you; I am with you. I love you. Come now and rest in Me. I will heal you of all your cares and concerns. Love Me. Love My People. Come and rest in Me.

Jesus,
yours forever."

August 5, 2010
Our Lord

"My dearest beloved of My Heart, my own, My Prophet, so desperately needed by the Church, now and forever, I greet you with love as King of Heaven and Earth, and dressed, as you see, in vibrant Priestly colors as Christ the King.

Woe to My Shepherds who do not listen to their people. Woe to them, for they will be judged harshly, for I anointed them as Priest to assist My Priestly People. They have not listened and obeyed. Woe to those who scoff at Me and say horrible things to My People. Judgement for them will be harsh. Will they recognize Me, when they see Me, if they cannot recognize Me now in My People? **This is sin. This is an abomination of the heart.** This is not what I came to Earth to be for My People.

I lay down and gave all of Me to My People, on a cross. I gave everything so they could be saved.

This is why My People are to be Me to each other. I know them and they follow Me."

August 7, 2010
Our Blessed Mother

"This is not a call for the fainthearted, but for those whom Our Lord has chosen to be His Apostles, very dear and very intimate with Him. This is a call of great sacrifice, of total abandonment to God on everything, on everything.

This call is like the call of Moses, of Abraham, of St. Paul, to go out to all the world and save as many souls as you possibly can for Heaven, for the Lord.

This is not a call for the fainthearted. This is a call for direct power from God to His People.

January 11, 2011
Our Lord (with Our Blessed Mother)

"Be not afraid; I go before you always. Be at peace; I am with you.

You are correct. There is much deceiving going on. Many are not listening. Souls are being lost. MY PRIESTHOOD IS DESECRATED BY LARGE EGOS, COLD HEARTS, AND NO COMPASSION. All are facts. And where are My People to go if the Shepherd I have given them is not working for Me.

So many, Mary, so many need Me. Where will I find good Shepherds of My Flock. Where?

My dearest beloved, do not sorrow so; I am with you. I will protect Christ the King *[our home parish]*. I know My People; they have not abandoned Me; they are wandering. I will send them a Shepherd to care for them.

Oh, My beloved, how My Heart aches for My People. Stay open, stay alert, I will ask of you more. I will speak again.

Our Lord"

January 20, 2011
Our Blessed Mother

"Many of God's People mean well, but the Shepherds of God's Flock have given up the fight. They are tired, lonely from God, and just want a peaceful last years, no worries, no problems, nothing to break their own life. God is not happy, for they do not complete all He has asked of them, all He has asked of them.

Do not become discouraged or worry about anything. God is watching over everything for you; your surrender is all He needs.

Your Mother Mary – All things belong to God"

April 2, 2011
Our Lord

"Thank you for loving My People so much, for your patience under stress, for you and your husband's understanding that I am in charge of My Priests. I will take care of them. Each Priest earning their time with Me, their Judge and Jury. It is not necessary for man to be judge of the souls. I AM HE. I AM THE JUDGE OF THE SOUL. Let all be given to Me. I will know what to do with it. Love Me. Love My Commandments. Love My People. All else I will take care of for you.

It is good, your/our home renovation. Keep all simple, for My Home was simplicity; this one with you should be kept the same. I am pleased with *** and your husband and their efforts to be in My Home and make it what I, your Lord and Savior, desire it to be: simple, lovely, prayerful at all times.

Go now, to love Me and serve My People. I remain yours forever.

Jesus,
Savior of the World, Lover of all mankind"

April 5, 2011
Our Lord

"I am watching over My Priests. All is not as humans see, does God see. I remain the Judge of all mankind. There is much for man to learn from God, very much for man to learn."

July 4, 2011
Our Blessed Mother

"My dearest daughter, how My Heart aches today for Priests. So many are lost, wandering, so many, so many. I have come so often to mankind to assist souls, souls of God's Priests, Bishops, souls of God's People, every rank of life, every lifestyle known to man.

Where has the world gone with the knowledge of Our Lord, His Dying on the Cross to save them, each of them He has died for."

September 18, 2011
Our Blessed Mother

"My dearest daughter of Our Lord Jesus Christ, I am here to tell you, we lost our Priest; He did not make it to Purgatory. We thank you for your prayers and listening. Remember always, God is the Judge, there is a Heaven, there is a Hell, there is Justice for all with God.

Remember always the dangers of sin, the gift of Free Will, given by God to assist man on Earth.

This is a tragic soul lost because he chose to hate God and to hate his call from God. This is an irreversible sin, so much so when man, who is given many opportunities to repent does not do so. The end is harsh but justified by God.

Rest now in the comfort that The Mass you offered for him and the extra prayers and sacrifices helped another Priest attain his reward in Heaven."

October 18, 2011
God the Father

"Do not be discouraged. I AM WHO AM. THERE IS NO OTHER. I AM HE. Believe and go forward with joy.

I will take care of you. I have heard your prayers of supplication for My People. As I spoke to Moses, I speak to you. As I blessed

Moses on his journey, I bless you. This is a journey of love and togetherness with Heaven. Be stouthearted and wait for the Lord. He will do everything for you.

Be at peace. I am pleased with you. When you pray, I pray. When you speak, I speak. When you are joyful, I am joyful, and when I see you sad, I am sad. My People need Me; they have Me in you.

Be at peace, all will be for the Greater Honor and Glory of God, all will be.

Stay with Me now as I also sorrow for My People, with you. I have heard their cries. I will assist them. I will send HOLY PRIESTS TO COMFORT THEM.

BE AT PEACE. I AM GOD. THERE IS NO OTHER. You must go now. Come and share each moment with Me. All will be as I have said it would be. I have spoken.

God the Father, beloved by you. Generations stand with you. Remain in Me forever."

January 26, 2013
Our Lord

"My Priests are in great need. My Shepherds have stopped loving as they need to love. My Shepherds have stepped back, not forward as I ask them to do for Me, their Lord and Savior.

We, in Heaven, are pleased with all efforts toward Father and the new Bishop meeting to share. This is My Church of Love. This is My Church of Love. This is My Church of Love. Love it as I do. Love Me forever.

Jesus,
Savior of the World, forever here with you,
Forever here with you."

February 27, 2013
Our Lord

"My Priests do not realize the great significance of their call as a Priest in the Order of Melchizedek.

There is a serious war for souls going on. Your lives are most important in this struggle to save as many souls as possible."

April 29, 2013
Our Lord

"All of Revelation is true, as spoken by St. John, all of Corinthians is true, all of the Gospels are true and on and on. My Priests have been told to question, to question, to be filled with anxiety: 'Did this really, truly happen? Is this truly the Body and Blood of Jesus? What can I truly believe?' they ask.

They are so in need of peace, peace of heart, peace in their souls that walking with their Lord is worth it. Are they doing any good for their People? Why are their people not attending Mass regularly? What is the answer?

The answer is your yes to Me."

May 12, 2013
Our Blessed Mother

"My dearest daughter, pray for Priests, so in need, so in need. Our Lord is saddened today at their hardness of heart. Many are allowing God's People to stray dangerously to the satanic suggestion of perversion, not only of heart, but perversion of soul. With this comes all types of sin, all affecting the mind of God's People.

Pray intense prayer for all, as the world has become very depraved."

July 18, 2013
Our Lord

"Do not be afraid but go forward day by day with Me. Do not count the hours, do not be afraid to speak up about the needs of My People, always bearing in your heart, My Heart, for My People.

Yes, there are My Priests aching for changes, bored with their People, but I, their Lord and God, I say to them, give Me everything. I can, and will, assist you. I know My People. I know My People."

October 9, 2013
Our Lord

"Oh, how My Heart aches for My Priests, so many caught in their world of demands of their people. Where am I – in their midst, assisting them. So many decide against Me and for the People. When will it end, you ask?

Come, assist Me with more souls. Your sacrificing today will gain Me souls."

October 15, 2013
Our Lord

"My Priests have so much sorrow, so much agony of heart. Pray for them daily and lay them at the foot of the Cross of Salvation.

Stay with Me, as we go now to assist My Priests so close to My Heart. Be open, be alert for communication from Heaven day or night. We love you and are with you on everything.

Your Beloved Jesus,
so in love with My Priests, in My Church, so in need, so in need."

January 2, 2014
Our Lord, Sacred Heart of Jesus, with St. Cloud (Patron of the city and Diocese of St. Cloud, MN)

"My dear couple, pray daily for My Priests. Offer your lives in supplication for My Priests, all of My Priests, all of My Priests.

The world has taken over their hearts, enfolded them in fear, in ignorance, in apathy. Their hearts, the hearts I created, the hearts I individually gave them, the hearts I so yearn, for them to return to Me, fully and completely.

My dearest beloved of My Heart, your call from Me is to offer up your life day by day for Me, day by day for Me, for My Priests. I will take anything you can give Me, anything. I will use it for My Priests and their salvation, for My Priests, and their salvation.

Today, offer up all for MY PRIESTS. I accept all you give Me. Come, let us go now together, today from this hour, and pray for My Priests.

Your beloved,
Jesus"

February 10, 2014
Our Lord

"My beloved, how pleased we are with you, always listening, eager to be all you can be, for Me, your Lord and Savior. I AM HERE FOR YOU, ALWAYS AND FOREVER.

Yes, continue praying for My Priests, those who are working, those who are dying, those who are refusing to accept My Call for them, those arrogant enough to think that I do not exist for them.

My dearest beloved, I need you. I need you for My Priests' salvation. Anything you can give to Me to assist Me, I will take. This is truly a high call, a much-needed call. All will be for the Honor and Glory of God, all will be.

Continue on, oh good and faithful servants; I am with you on everything. My love now as you go to rest.

Your beloved,
Jesus, forever and ever yours."

April 1, 2014
Our Lord

"Yes, your brother, Fr. *** is with Me, enjoying the fruits of his labors. Yes, rejoice and be glad you have another Saint ready to do battle for you, for your family; again, I say rejoice.

For today, offer up all pain, all annoyances, all anxiety, all sorrow for My Priests who labor with love to My People. Keep all of them in prayer, all of them. Go now to rest a bit before Mass. I am with you.

Your Beloved Jesus,
forever and ever with you."

July 22, 2014
Our Blessed Mother

"Offer up everything for Priests to return to the Lord, as they need to, as He asks of them. Day and night. He asks this of them. Why then do they insist on living life their way, ONLY their way?

Be attentive to the promptings of Our Lord and His desires of you. HIS TIMING IS EVERYTHING. HE IS. THERE IS NO OTHER.

Be still then, and wait for the Lord to lead, then follow.

Your Mother Mary,
With Her Son Jesus Christ,
For all and forever."

July 27, 2014
God The Father

"My dearest beloved of My Heart, My Mother's Heart, this is God the Father asking of you the greatest sacrifice, **to die to self and live only in Me.** This is your call, to be all of Me to My People, all of Me. This My People need: all of Me. So desperately do they work for the world, when their only desire should be to work for Me. **This is the ultimate sacrifice: to be Me to My People.**

Now today, open your minds and hearts to a new beginning with Me, leaving all to be all to My People. Only in Me can you succeed, for this is a direct call from God. Nothing now should matter to you but Me, nothing.

I will show you where to go, with whom. I will lead you to the place I need you at for My needs of My People. Follow Me, fully trusting that all will be for the Honor and Glory of God, all will be.

My love, with My Mother.
God the Father, God the Son, God the Holy Spirit."

July 27, 2014
Our Blessed Mother

"My most beloved servants of the Lord, you have given your lives fully to the Lord. There is no mountain that cannot be climbed. There is no ocean that you cannot swim. There is no barrier holding you from doing the will of the Lord, your treasure.

Listen carefully when I ask this of you: will you sacrifice for the next two days so My Priests, My Beloved Priests, can have some relief? Their lives have become laden down with worldly interests. How can I bring them back and closer to the Lord? I need you both and the sacrifices you can offer to God for them.

Be open, be alert, and continue on in your ordered tasks in your home. God will direct you as to how He desires your lives to be. HE IS. THERE IS NO OTHER. I will leave you now to rest in the Lord. God's Peace, God's Love, God's Joy be with you.
Your Mother Mary,
Queen of Heaven and Earth, Queen of Peace

Love All My People, forever and ever, Amen."

August 9, 2014
Our Lord

"My dearest beloved, come and sit with Me. This is a very tough time for My Priests. They are being used and abused by My People, some of them are in high positions of the Diocese.

Come together with your Bishop, our Bishop, and discuss what can be done to assist them. The laity have been misguided, so now it needs a Bishop's touch to reeducate them as to the duties of a Priest of God, especially Diocesan Priests ordained to work with their Bishop for His People.

This is a great agony of heart for Me, their Lord and Savior. How can My Priests be loved as they are to be loved. They are not a god and should not be treated with abuse and vile language.

My Priests are called by Me, their Savior, and no one will take that call away from them. They are to be Me to My People, yet some need to learn how to love as I love.

Be open then to finishing the tasks I have asked of you. Do not worry or negate any of it, but be joyful as I am joyful. Come now, and let us begin.

Yours forever,
Jesus, King of Heaven and Earth, King of Peace forever."

August 18, 2014
Our Lord

"My dearest couple, so close to My Heart, this is a time of great sorrow. There are still Priests wanting their own way in life, doing their own thing, their own decisions and not obeying those I have chosen to direct them. Where did I, their Lord, go wrong? Is there nowhere I can lay My Head, My Heart, at rest?

Come now, My dearest couple, close to My Heart, and stay with Me awhile. Come....

My dear couple, pray for Priests that they will surrender their will to My Will for them. Go to rest now and pray.

Your Beloved Jesus,
forever yours, always with My Priests, always"

October 17, 2014
Our Blessed Mother

"I am here tonight to ask again for more prayers for My Priests, so in need, so in need. The world has been crucifying them and this sadly will continue. We need you for prayer for them to stay devoted to God and their Priestly Call.

Our Love,
Your Mother Mary, Queen of Peace with all in Heaven"

October 18, 2014
Our Lord

"My Hand is taking care of My Priests as I give each of them My love, My peace, My Joy. Do not worry anymore. All will now flow for the good of My Priests so in need, so in need.

Your beloved, now and forever,
Jesus, yours forever."

July 22, 2015
Our Lord

"Stay focused on My Priests, My Catholic Priests who have learned to desecrate all that is Holy. They have learned to believe heretical views and opinions of even some of the highest-ranking officials in the Church, My Church, so badly beaten and ridiculed and made fun of. Where do they, who have the voices, receive their information?

Be open, be alert, I need you now and forever. Be ready now to take on the forces of evil in a battle that will make Me, King of Heaven and Earth, Jesus Christ, Savior of the world, TRIUMPHANT.

My love forever,
Jesus, King of Heaven and Earth"

August 29, 2015
Our Lord and Blessed Mother

"Pray for Priests today. So many are caught in the worldly distractions, so many. Where are My Apostles for the end times? Where are they?

Come now, let us pray together for My Priests, My beloved Priests, who stay so close to Me and say yes to all of My requests. Let us pray for My Priests.

Continue on, oh good and faithful servants. You will always know where I want you, what I desire of you for My People. You will always know and be at peace.

With sadness, Fr. *** did not make Purgatory or Heaven. If you ask it of Me, I would ask for more prayer and penances *[for him to save his soul]*, but he chose to be god, writing his own rules for his own church. Yes, in blatant view of his fellow Clergy Brothers. What happened? His heart grew cold and he decided to do things his way, but voluntarily and viciously defied Church authority.

My beloved, we say this to you, so you know how serious a call to My Priesthood is, and how hard satan is working to defy God. Be open, be alert, for I need you, I need you to assist My Priests in many ways necessary for them so they remain solid in the Faith of Jesus Christ, solid in The Catholic Church.

Be aware then of the great apostasy, the heretics roaming freely, eager to destroy My People, My so in need People.

This then, do for Me: pray earnestly that My Priests will stay the course, remain steadfast, and are open to die for their faith in Me, God Almighty.

I will go now; rest in Me.
Your Beloved Jesus, forever and ever, yours.
My Love Forever."

October 17, 2015
Our Lord, to His Priests

"Do not worry about Fr. ***, who came through a tough time of suffering.

This is but a passing moment in life. I will repay you, all of you, a hundredfold for your tenacity of faith, courage under stress, and patience that only I can fully bless. MY HAND IS UPON HIM. HE WILL CONQUER ALL I ASK OF HIM. HE IS MINE. I AM HIS. This truly is living the Gospel. May we have more Priests doing the same. I BLESS YOU IN THE NAME OF THE FATHER, AND OF THE SON, AND OF THE HOLY SPIRIT, AMEN, forever and ever, Amen."

December 2, 2015
Our Lord, weeping for His Priesthood

"My beloved, pray for My Priesthood, pray for My Priesthood. Never in the history of mankind has there ever been a great movement to crush My Priesthood as nothing, holding no significance.

Protestantism has driven it to a breaking point: people believe all Priests are just men in a career call who have no significant difference to their chaplains, their own named people. Yes, they also have women in this position.

Mary, My Beloved, I call you to a new adventure with Me. My People need to know the significance of the Priesthood as I instituted it. Be open then to educating My People. Be open then to the exhausting, but very much needed, call to go out to My People. You can no longer be a daily contemplative. I need you now as you, as a holy couple, together with Me; we will assist My People.

The Sacredness of the call to My Priesthood, the Sacredness of The Sacrament of Holy Orders, must be continued as I created My Church for My People.

I leave you for a moment, go and teach My People, I ask this of you.

Jesus,
your beloved, always here for you"

December 31, 2015
Our Lord

"Stay with Me, stay with Me, pray for My Catholic Priests so enamored with the world. Pray they may have the strength to combat the evil one who is prowling around seeking their souls.

Yes, of all the people who go to Hell, My Priests are with them. Pray hard so we may save more of them from perdition. Go to pray, and be at rest now. I am with you, for always."

January 6, 2016
Our Blessed Mother: Queen of Peace, Queen of the Holy Rosary, Queen of Heaven and Earth

"My dear couple of God, how we rejoice with you that God blessed humankind with suffering. You have entered the realm of the Holy Spirit that only a few can enter and follow through on all God is asking of them. Rejoice, you have been allowed into this realm of glory and praise to God, forever and ever, Amen. Forever and ever, Amen.

Go today, offering up all of this tooth pain for Priests who have desecrated the Holy Eucharist. Some will listen and obey their Bishops, but some are arrogantly following their own way, not God's Way.

Listen carefully as I say this to you, God will always tell you explicitly what He desires of you. Stay with Us. We are with you on everything.

Your Mother Mary,
Queen of all, Queen of your hearts"

January 20, 2016
Our Lord (with St. Michael the Archangel)

"My dearest beloved, pray hard for My Priests, so in need of Me, so in need of Me. Where are My Bishops to console them? Where are they, busying themselves with other things not of the soul? Where are My Bishops?

Stay with Me awhile tonight; My Priests need Me, they need Me. Go to rest; pray with Me, My beloved; I need you to pray for My Priests.

Jesus,
Savior of the World"

September 7, 2016
Our Lord

"My dear couple, keep in prayer three Priests struggling with so much anger, frustration; and they are not bringing their problems to Me. I desire their prayers, their yearning of the heart. I am with you today, as always. Stay focused on Me and My Calls to you both. All will be for the Honor and Glory of God, all will be."

December 11, 2016
Our Lord

"Stay close to Me today; many Priests, Catholic Priests, are in deep need; very much has been thrown at them by My people raised from birth in the Catholic Faith. These of My People are the worst, as they cannot seem to grasp the grave importance of Honoring Me, Respecting Me, their Lord and Savior.

Mary, My beloved, spend time in prayer for My Priests, My beloved Priests.

Your beloved Jesus,
always here for you."

* * * * * * *

As we were publishing this volume, Mary felt the Lord wanted the following message to be added, even though it is a more recent message:

November 19, 2019
An Angel
"For His Priests, HIS BELOVED CATHOLIC PRIESTS"

Our Lord
THE SORROWFUL MYSTERIES

The Agony in the Garden – You, My Priest, were in the Garden of Gethsemane, WITH ME. IN MY AGONY, WE WERE TOGETHER.

Scourging at the Pillar – You, My Priest, you were with Me at the Scourging Pillar. We suffered together, you and I, WE SUFFERED TOGETHER.

Crowning with Thorns – My Priest, you are Me to My People, YOU ARE ME, therefore, you carry daily a crown of thorns from My People, suffering for each of them. I am not alone, we carry this crown of thorns together.

Carrying of The Holy Cross of Salvation – FOR ALL MY PEOPLE, you, My Priest carry multiple crosses, for My People. You are not alone, WE CARRY THE CROSSES, TOGETHER. We, together, you and I, we suffer together.

The Crucifixion – You, My Priest, are ON THE CROSS WITH ME. You are hanging on the Cross With Me. WE ARE TOGETHER. We are together, forever. I love you.

My Priest, come and walk with Me, give Me, everything, all Joys and Sorrows. We are together, forever. I love you."

Messages from Heaven: For My Priests continues in *Messages From Heaven: For My Priests, Vol. II* (coming soon!), and there are Messages specifically for the lay people of God in *Messages from Heaven: For My People.*

We hope that you will reflect on what God has spoken to your heart as you have read this book. God indeed wants your soul with Him in Heaven for all of eternity. Do not be afraid to commit all of your heart, all of your mind, all of your soul, all of your strength, to Him in love every day.

God's Call to the priesthood is a unique and precious call. May you be encouraged in your Calling and not be afraid to share your faith. For the salvation of souls is the mission of every disciple!

You are loved.

Acknowledgements

We give great thanks to Our Lord for all His many blessings in our daily lives. Also, deep gratitude is owed to:

Bishop Donald Kettler, who encourages us to prayerfully follow through as the Lord requests. Our Spiritual Directors for their prayers and support. Our daughter and son-in-law, DeAnna and Michael Parks, for their help in editing and publishing these books, including the cover design.

Our Priest sons, Fathers Aaron and Matthew Kuhn, who, in addition to their heavy parish duties, still find time to support us in prayer and wisdom.

And to all those who offered their advice and counsel on how to best publish these messages: Thank you for your great support!

About the Authors

Greg and Mary Kuhn are best known for work in Jesus Heals Ministry and hospital ministry in the Diocese of Saint Cloud, MN. They have been married for over 45 years. Mr. & Mrs. Kuhn have two sons who are Roman Catholic priests and a daughter who is married with three beautiful daughters and works in film and parish ministries.

Mrs. Kuhn has received messages from Our Lord since she was a child, but it was only in 1993 that she was asked to write them down. In 2016, Greg and Mary were asked by God to begin publishing these messages. For more information on these books, and others Greg and Mary have written, please visit www.SufferingHearts.org.

Other books by Greg & Mary Kuhn:

Messages from Heaven: For My People, Vol. I

Messages from Heaven: For My People, Vol. II (Coming Summer 2021)